Newly - Revised
Realistic Duck Carving

A Step by Step Illustrated Manual
by Alfred M. Ponte

Publisher: Alan Giagnocavo
Project Editor: Ayleen Stellhorn
Desktop Specialist: Robert Altland, Altland Design

Special thanks to Willie McDonald of the Duck Blind for the reference photos that appear on the covers.

ISBN# 1–56523–086–8

Newly revised *Realistic Duck Carving: A Step-by-Step Illustrated Manual* by Alfred M. Ponte. Previous editions copyrighted by Bird Sculptures in Wood; First Printing, November 1981; Second Printing, January 1982; Third Printing, January 1983; Fourth Printing, December 1983; Fifth Printing, April 1986; Sixth Printing, May 1993; Seventh Printing, June 1995.

To order your copy of this book,
please send check or money order
for $9.95 plus $2.50 shipping to:
Fox Books Orders
Box 7948
Lancaster, PA 17604–7948

Dedication

First and foremost, I dedicate this book to my Lord and Savior, Jesus Christ.

To my five children, Michelle, David, Sandie, Brenda and Kevin,
who were always ready with their encouragement.
Above all to my wonderful wife, Carol, who not only suggested the idea of the book,
but who has typed the many rough drafts, made numerous phone calls and ran errands everywhere.
She also encouraged me when I wondered if I should go on,
gently prodded me when it was necessary, and has had undying faith in me.

A WORD ABOUT THE AUTHOR

Al Ponte's lifelong interest in the preservation and study of waterfowl and songbirds took a creative turn when he began carving. Since then, his abilities have been recognized by wood carvers throughout the United States. By helping to introduce this American art form to others, Al is, in a way, expressing his thanks for his special talents.

This book of instructions is a formal effort to enable others to experience some of his personal enjoyment of wood carving. It is lacking only in the warmth and enjoyment one derives from being fortunate enough to be his student.

W. T. Schrift

Al Ponte, well-known wood carver, is like most good artists. He is critical of his work and strives for realism and perfection. His ambition is to be among the best bird carvers in the world and this gives him the patience to do his research well and use every available reference, so as to counterfeit the live specimen.

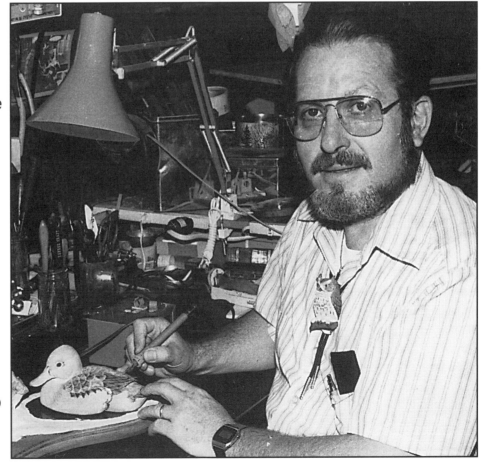

His students find him demanding, but patient. His criticism is coupled with praise and encouragement.

We often admire the superb work of other carvers and wonder how they do it so well. We dismiss the possibility that it was hard work, learning by trial and error. We feel the artist has a natural ability, and just carved a masterpiece the first time. Nothing is further from the truth. There is no substitute for frustration in the learning process, but it can be reduced by listening to the artist and following his instructions carefully. Soon your own creativity takes over and you can carve your own masterpiece.

With these foolproof directions and step-by-step instructions Al has simplified carving a duck.

Richard A. Solmen

TABLE OF CONTENTS

INTRODUCTION

After my own struggles as a beginner bird carver and watching other beginners and my own students struggle to achieve a realistic duck carving, I decided that a simplified method was needed.

I, therefore, spent the next five years improving my method until I arrived at what I consider to be a fool-proof approach.

If followed carefully, step-by-step, this book will provide you with a surefire way to carve a realistic duck, which will surprise even the first-time carver.

The pattern in this book is that of a ¾ size Lesser Scaup (Bluebill). Although the illustrations in the book reflect a Bluebill, this method applies to most species of ducks by merely using a different pattern. Additional patterns are included for your future use.

One of my favorite sayings is, "It takes an inch of talent and a yard of perseverance to succeed in any endeavor." This truly applies to carving.

It is my sincere wish that this book will open the door to a very rewarding experience and years of pleasure derived from bird carving.

Your carving friend,
Alfred M. Ponte

TOOLS RECOMMENDED FOR THIS PROJECT

 1. X-ACTO™ KNIFE & NO 11 BLADE

 2. LIGHT DUTY KNIFE

 3. HEAVY DUTY KNIFE

 4. 1/8" V-GOUGE

 5. 5/16" SKEW CHISEL

 6. 1/4" U-GOUGE

 7. BURNING TOOL

 8. PENCIL

9. BAND SAW

10. 1/4" AND 1/16" DRILL BITS AND DRILL

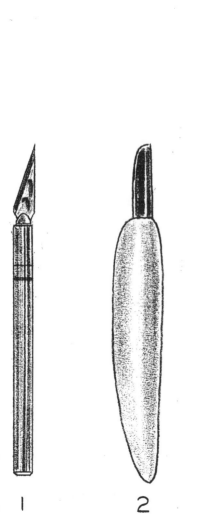
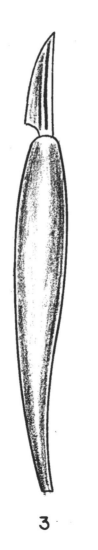

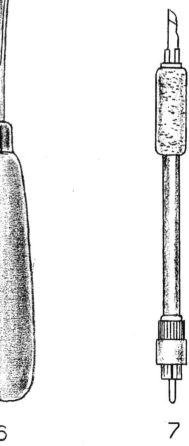

2

1 2 3 4 5 6 7

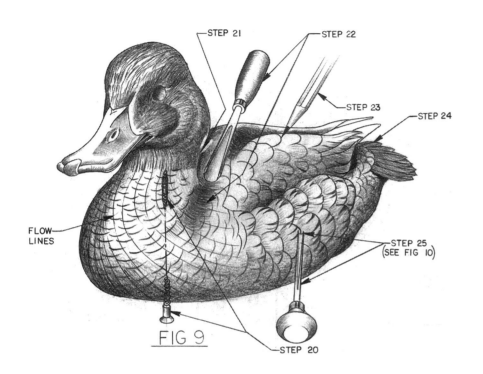

STEP 21 STEP 22 STEP 23 STEP 24

STEP 25
(SEE FIG 10)

FLOW
LINES

FIG 9

STEP 20

Materials List

8 1/4" x 4 1/2" x 2 1/2" basswood block
4" x 2" x 2" basswood block
clear plastic vinyl
scissors
compass, height gauge or ruler
two-part quick setting epoxy
double-ended wood screw or long wood screw
8mm yellow glass eyes
wood filler
lacquer-based sanding sealer
gesso
stiff tooth brush
acrylic paints
paint brushes

Safety First

Before getting started we want to urge you to develop good safety practices any time you are using any type of woodworking machinery or hand tools, as well as good common sense when using finishes of any kind. Be sure to read and follow the manufacturer's safety recommendations for your power tools before you begin any woodworking project.

This is a picture of the finished three-quarter size Bluebill. Additional patterns can be found in the Pattern Treasury at the back of this book. Any of these patterns can be used with the carving method outlined in this book.

BAND SAWING AND DRILLING

Bandsawing

For the body, use a block of basswood thick enough to accommodate the side view template and wide enough to allow $1/4$" to spare on each side of the plan view template. To carve the $3/4$ size Bluebill featured in this book, you'd need a basswood block measuring approximately 8 $1/4$" x 4 $1/2$" x 2 $1/2$".

Follow the instructions on page 7 to make a template for the plan and side views of the body. Lay out the plan view by tracing around the template with a sharp pointed pencil. Come as close to the actual size of the pattern as possible. Then layout the side view. To make sure that the plan view and side view coincide with each other, make sure the tail touches the rear of the block in both views. See illustration A, page 6.

Start cutting the plan view with a band saw, stopping at the points indicated on the side of the body. See Illustration A, page 6. Back the blade out of the block. Cut from the opposite direction to a point about 1 $1/2$" away from the point at which you stopped in the previous cut. Repeat these steps on the other half of the body. Leaving a portion of the block uncut will allow you to maintain a solid block in order to band saw the side view, which is the next step.

Once the side view has been bandsawed, lay the block back on its bottom and complete the 1 $1/2$" cuts that held the wood together.

For the head you'll need a block of basswood measuring approximately 4" x 2" x 2". Only band saw the side view, making sure that the bill is in line with the grain.

Drilling

Lay the side view template for the head on the block and mark the eye and nostril locations. Using a drill press to ensure the locations are correct on both sides of the head, drill a $1/16$" diameter hole for the nostril and a $1/4$" hole for the eye. Make sure these holes go all the way through the blank. See Illustration D, page 6

In the case of the $1/16$" hole, since drills that small are usually rather short, make sure that you have drilled past the center line with this hole.

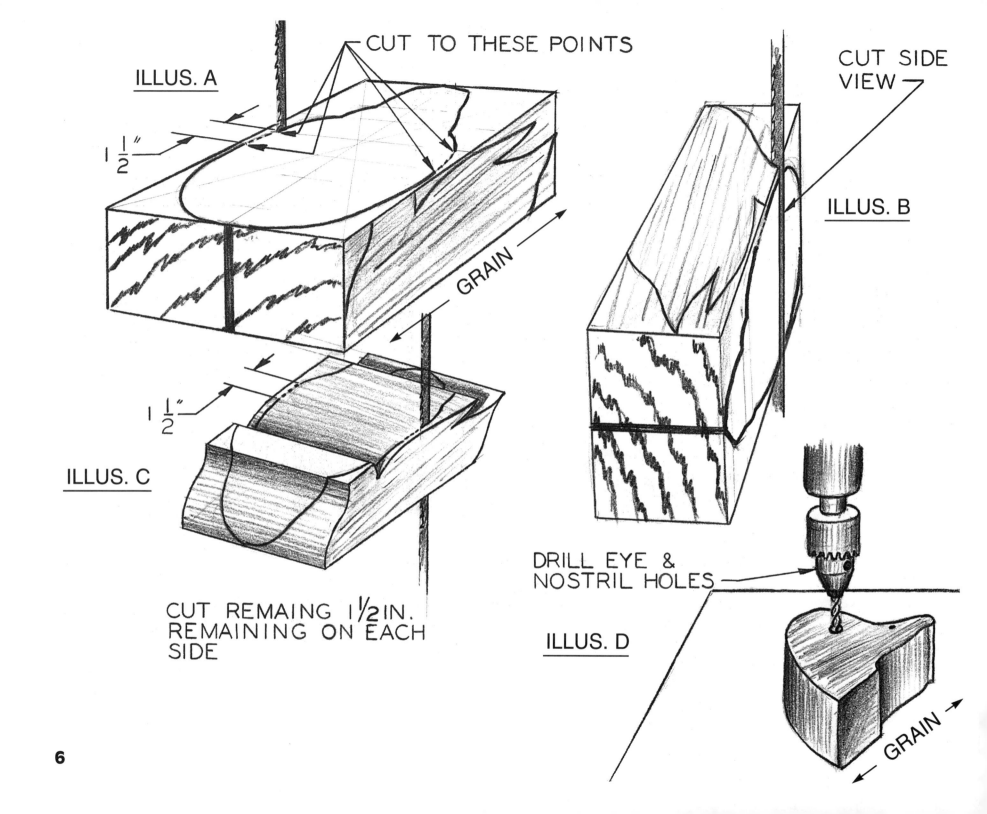

CUT TO THESE POINTS

ILLUS. A

$1\frac{1}{2}"$

GRAIN

CUT SIDE VIEW

ILLUS. B

ILLUS. C

$1\frac{1}{2}"$

CUT REMAING 1½IN.
REMAINING ON EACH
SIDE

DRILL EYE &
NOSTRIL HOLES

ILLUS. D

GRAIN

TEMPLATE INSTRUCTIONS

Trace all the information from the plan and side view drawings (pages 8 and 9) onto clear plastic vinyl approximately .010 of an inch thick. Trace the plan and side views of the body and the head separately. Take care to accurately trace the information, as any error at any stage can be compounded and ultimately give you a carving that is far from looking like the bird depicted in this book.

Add a center line to the plan view templates of the head and body.

The reason I use clear plastic for making my templates is that I can "sight" through the template to transfer the information to the block of wood.

Familiarize yourself with all the different names used on the drawings on pages 8 and 9. It will make your job considerably easier if you know what part of the bird is being referred to in the instructions.

The heavy lines on the drawings on pages 8 and 9 denote the different feather groups.

Once you have carefully traced all of the information from the drawings on pages 8 and 9 to a sheet of plastic, cut out each individual template with sharp scissors. You should have four templates: Plan View Body, Plan View Head, Side View Body, Side View Head. You'll also need a template for the side of the upper mandible.

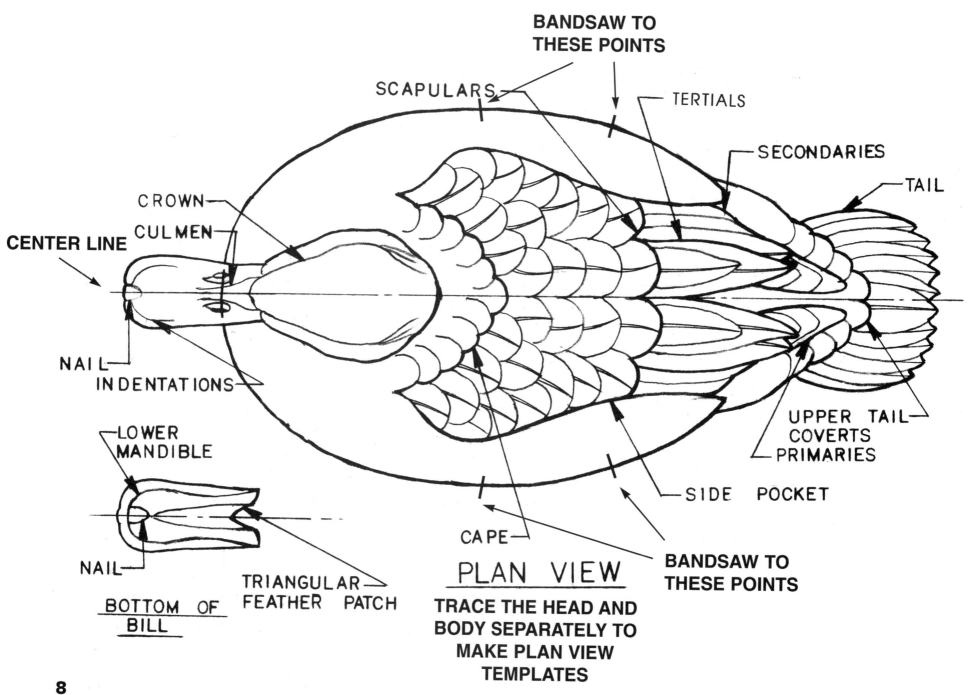

BANDSAW TO
THESE POINTS

SCAPULARS

TERTIALS

SECONDARIES

TAIL

CROWN

CULMEN

CENTER LINE

NAIL

INDENTATIONS

UPPER TAIL
COVERTS
PRIMARIES

LOWER
MANDIBLE

SIDE POCKET

NAIL

TRIANGULAR
FEATHER PATCH

CAPE

BOTTOM OF
BILL

PLAN VIEW

BANDSAW TO
THESE POINTS

TRACE THE HEAD AND
BODY SEPARATELY TO
MAKE PLAN VIEW
TEMPLATES

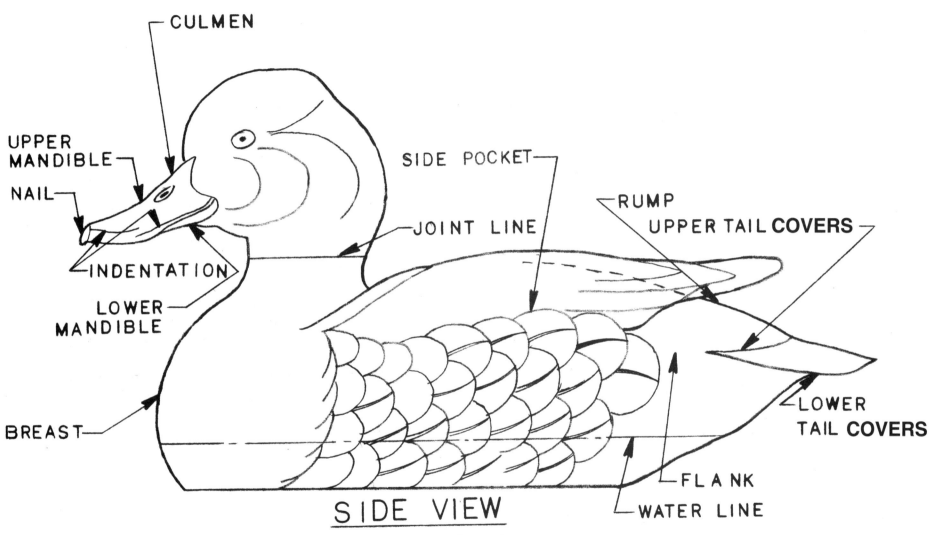

CULMEN

UPPER
MANDIBLE

NAIL

INDENTATION

LOWER
MANDIBLE

BREAST

SIDE POCKET

JOINT LINE

RUMP

UPPER TAIL **COVERS**

LOWER
TAIL **COVERS**

FLANK

WATER LINE

SIDE VIEW

**TRACE THE HEAD AND BODY SEPARATELY
TO MAKE SIDE VIEW TEMPLATES. MAKE AN
ADDITIONAL TEMPLATE OF THE SIDE OF
THE UPPER MANDIBLE.**

9

HEAD

Step 1   Draw a center line all around the head blank using a compass or a height gauge. You could also use a ruler to mark the center point in several places around the head and then connect the points with a flexible ruler. See Figure 1, page 11.

Step 2   Lining up the center line on the plan view template with the center line on the blank, lay the template on the surface of the bill and draw the outline. By laying the true view of the bill on the surface of the blank, it forces you to make the lines of the head go outboard sooner than normal. This will prevent you from running out of wood in the bill area. From the point on the block where the plan view of the bill ends and the head starts to go outward (Point A), free-hand a smooth arc to the widest outboard point on the top of the head (Point B). Then draw a large radius on each rear corner of the head. Do not necessarily follow the lines established by the plan view template. The following steps will cause everything to fall into place, if followed carefully. Refer again to Figure 1, page 11. Now using a heavy duty knife, cut out the plan view of the head.

Step 3   Draw the crown. Pick the widest points on the crown (Points C) and draw a wide arc from those points to the point on the center line where the bill and head meet (Point D). See Figures 2 and 2A , page 11.

Step 4   Draw lines for the rear and bottom of the upper mandible. Draw a line through the eye hole for use in Step 5. See Figure 2, page 11.

PLAN VIEW OF HEAD

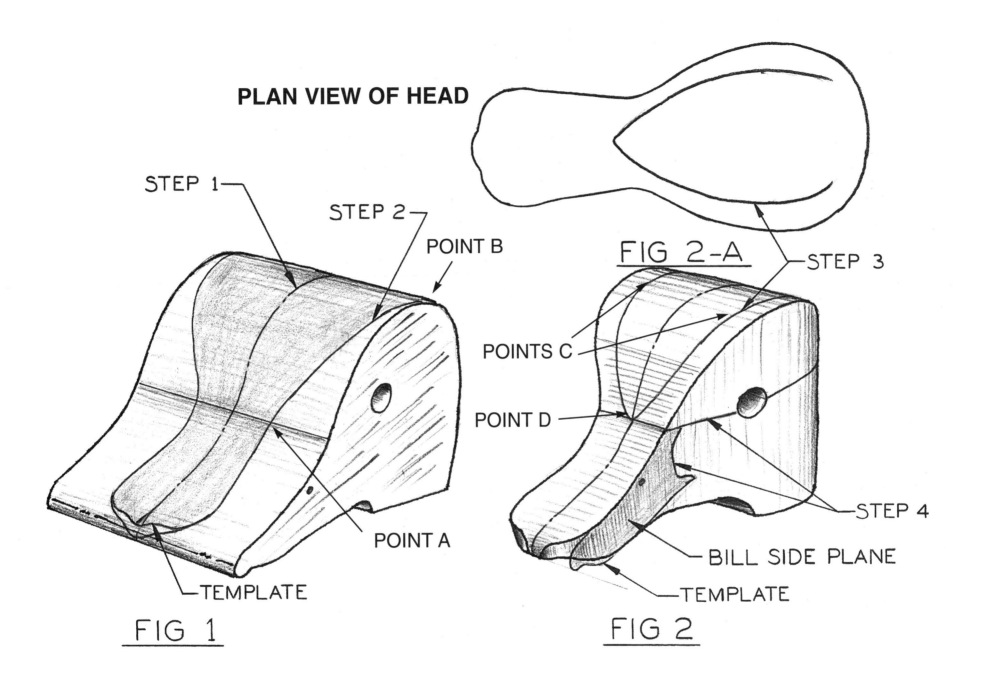

STEP 1

STEP 2

POINT B

POINT A

TEMPLATE

FIG 1

FIG 2-A

STEP 3

POINTS C

POINT D

STEP 4

BILL SIDE PLANE

TEMPLATE

FIG 2

Step 5   Carve down from the crown line and in from the line through the eye until your cuts intersect. This will create a 90-degree step. See Figure 3, page 13.

 Step 6   Make an incision perpendicular to the center line along the rear edge and bottom of the upper mandible. Slowly remove the wood by thin layers until the bill side plane and incision intersect. See Figure 3, page 13.

 Step 7   In the same manner as the previous step, expose the lower mandible. See Figure 4, page 13.

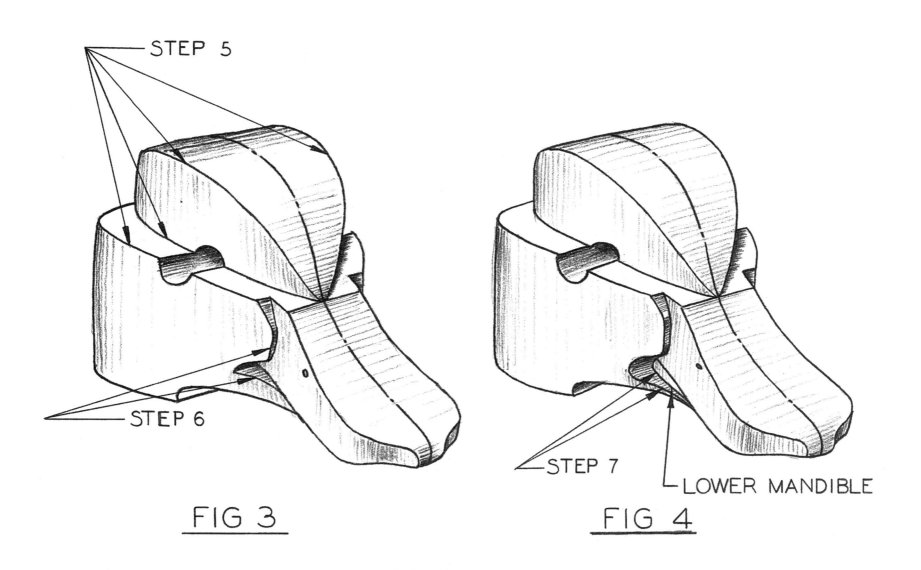

STEP 5

STEP 6

STEP 7

LOWER MANDIBLE

FIG 3

FIG 4

13

Step 8   Using the drawing of the bottom of the bill from page 8, draw the outline of the lower mandible. See Figure 5, page 15.

Step 9   Remove the remaining triangular web below the lower mandible. See Figure 6, page 15.

Step 10   Draw a line on the side of the head, starting halfway up at the side of the upper mandible, arcing toward the rear of the head, through the bottom of the eye hole and blending in with the shelf created in Step 5. See Figure 6, page 15.

Step 11   Draw the culmen and nostrils, top and side, referring to the drawings on pages 8 and 9. See Figure 6, page 15. Draw the side lines of the nostrils perpendicular to the top of the bill.

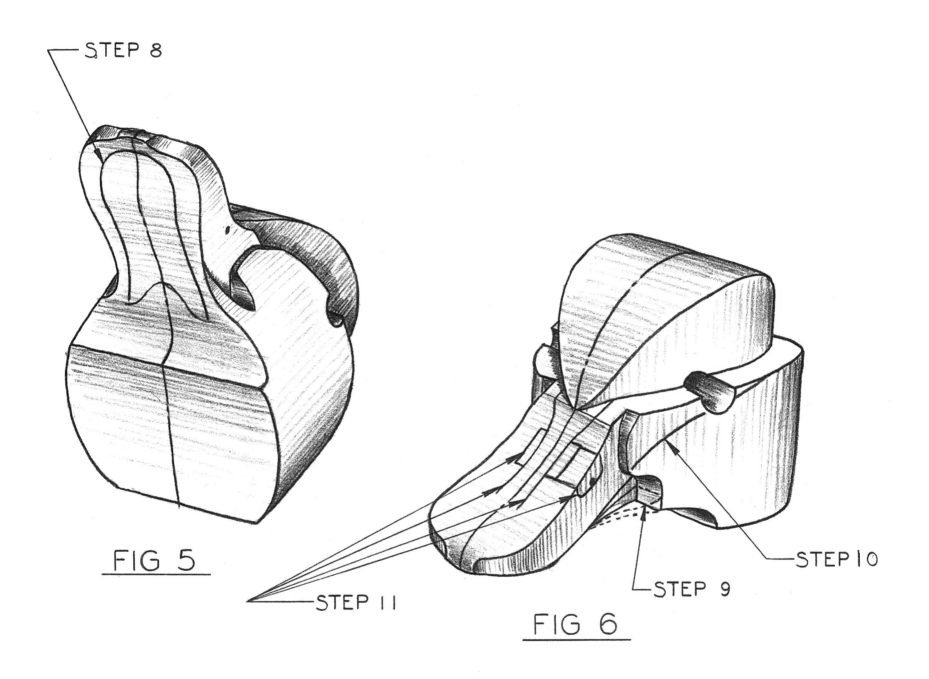

STEP 8

FIG 5

STEP 11

STEP 9

STEP 10

FIG 6

15

Step 12 With a carving knife, separate the lower mandible from the upper mandible. Define the triangular feather patch below the lower mandible. See Figure 7, page 17.

 Step 13 Create the nostril plane by first making a vertical cut along the plan view nostril line. Make a second cut following the side view nostril line. Remove the wood until the horizontal and vertical planes intersect. See Figure 8, page 17.

Round off the crown and rear of the head. See Figure 9, page 19. Take care not to, at this point, shape the bottom of the head. It will be shaped after it is fastened to the body.

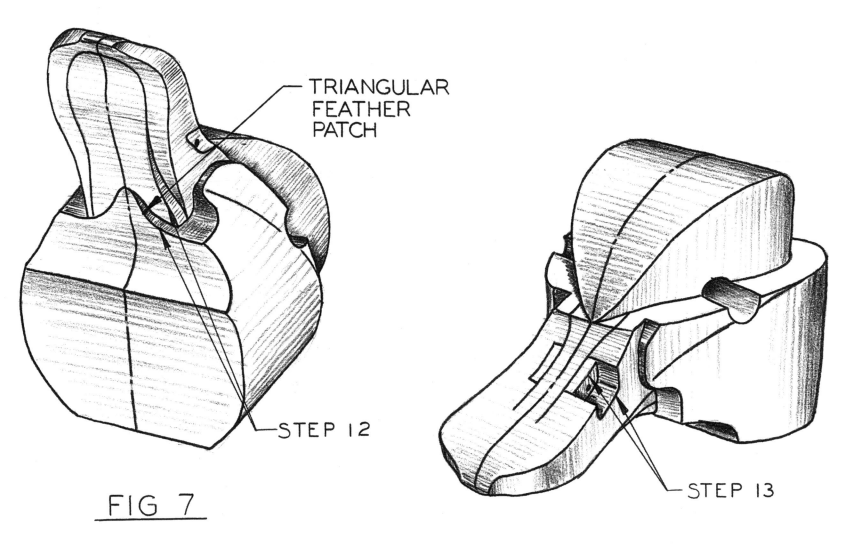

TRIANGULAR
FEATHER
PATCH

STEP 12

FIG 7

STEP 13

FIG 8

Step 14   Starting at the rear of the culmen line and arcing outward and downward, create an "S" curve to the bottom of the upper mandible. See Figure 9, page 19 and Figure 10, page 21. Round off the bill, maintaining a crisp line along the culmen and rolling all bill surfaces toward the nostrils.

Step 15   Draw and create the slot for the nostril. See Figure 9, page 19.

Step 16   Draw all pertinent lines on the lower mandible and completely separate the upper mandible from the lower mandible. Carve detail on the lower mandible. See Section A-A, Figures 9A and 9B, page 19.

Step 17   Using a U-gouge, follow the line established in Step 10, from the rear of the upper mandible through the eye. Carefully remove thin layers of wood to the depth indicated in Figure 9, page 19. Take care to leave a step, as shown in Figure 9, as a flat surface. (See also Figure 10, page 21.) For safety's sake, you may want to mount the head on a holding device so as to have both hands on the gouge.

Step 18   Round off the nostrils down to the edge of the nostril slot. Draw lines for the nail and indentations as shown in Figure 9, page 19. Using a small V-gouge, follow these lines to create a small "ditch." See Section A-A, page 19.

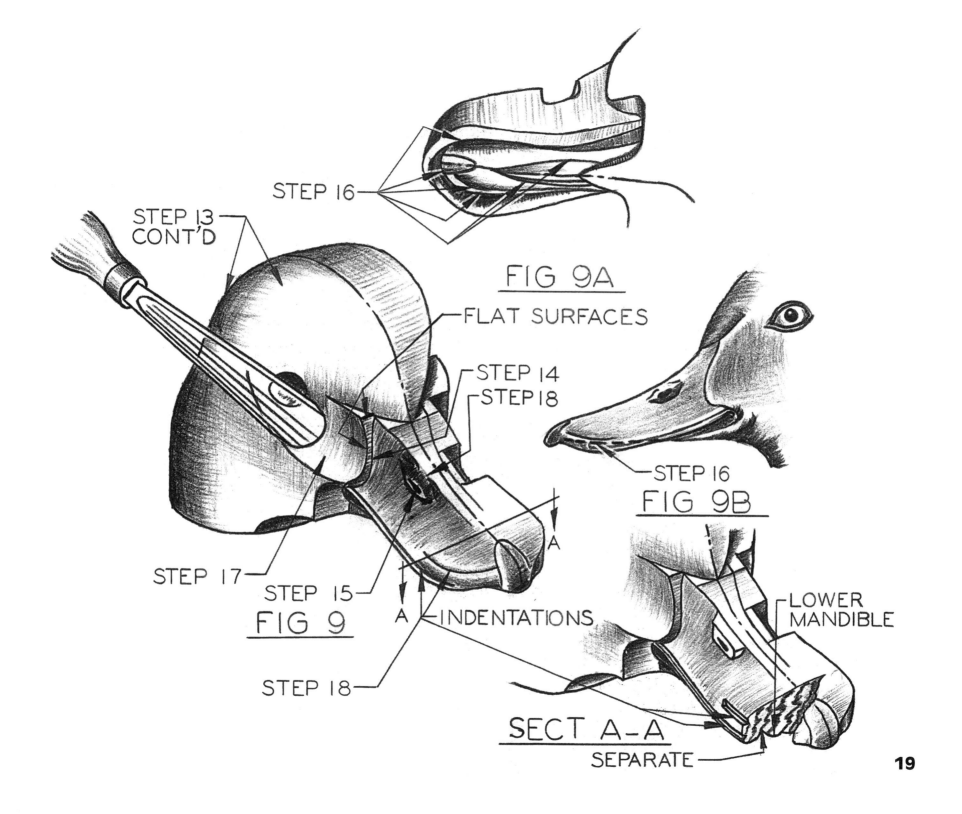

STEP 16

FIG 9A

FLAT SURFACES

STEP 13 CONT'D

STEP 14
STEP 18

STEP 16

FIG 9B

STEP 17

STEP 15

FIG 9

STEP 18

A

A

INDENTATIONS

LOWER MANDIBLE

SECT A-A

SEPARATE

19

Step 19   Round off the indentations, bill and nail to the center of the ditch created in Step 18. See Figure 11 and Section B-B, page 21.

 Step 20   Starting at the upper rear corner of the culmen, draw a slightly arced line upward and outward, as shown in Figures 10 and 11, page 21. Create a crease on that line by first making a small "ditch" with a V-gouge. Then round off the sides toward the center of the ditch.

 Step 21   Round off all remaining squared-off areas, taking care not to obliterate the flat surface where the cheek meets the bill, still visible in Figure 9, page 19. (See Figure 10, page 21, for the basic front view shape of the head.) Again, take care not to shape the bottom of the head.

Step 22   Now round off the above-mentioned flat surface where the cheek meets the bill. See Figures 10 and 11, page 21.

 Step 23   Hollow out the eye area . The distance between the eyes should equal the widest point at the base of the bill. See Figure 10, page 21.

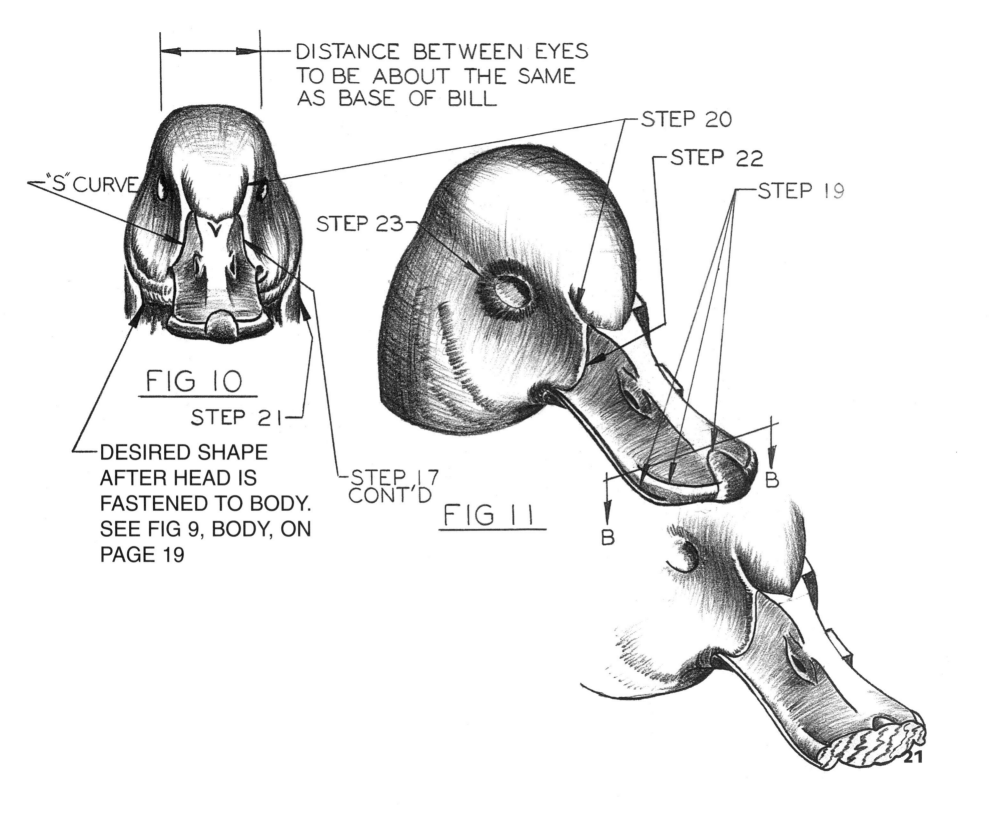

DISTANCE BETWEEN EYES
TO BE ABOUT THE SAME
AS BASE OF BILL

"S" CURVE

STEP 20

STEP 22

STEP 19

STEP 23

FIG 10

STEP 21

DESIRED SHAPE
AFTER HEAD IS
FASTENED TO BODY.
SEE FIG 9, BODY, ON
PAGE 19

STEP 17
CONT'D

FIG 11

B

B

21

BODY

 Step 1   Draw a center line around the length of the entire body, top and bottom. See Figure 1, page 23.

 Step 2   Using the side view template you created from the drawing on page 9, draw the side pocket line.

 Step 3   Plot a line halfway between the bottom and the top of the blank. See Line A, Figure 1, page 23. This will be the widest part of the body, according to its design.

BODY

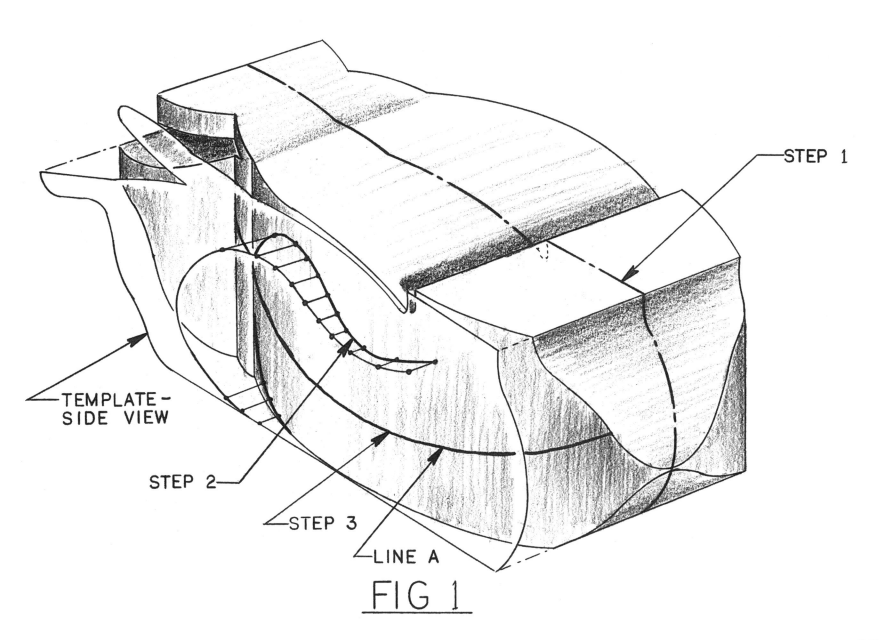

STEP 1

TEMPLATE - SIDE VIEW

STEP 2

STEP 3

LINE A

FIG 1

23

Step 4   Using the plan view template that you created based on the drawing on page 8, draw the side pocket. See Figure 2, page 25.

Step 5   With a draw knife, remove all the wood between the side pocket lines. This step enables you to remove excess wood prior to the next step. See Figure 3, page 26.

Note: Surforms, wood rasps or other tools may also be used.

Step 6   Make a vertical incision along the side pocket line drawn on the back of the Bluebill. Next, make a horizontal incision along the side pocket line drawn on the bird's side. Remove wood carefully until a 90-degree step or notch is created. See Figure 4, page 27. The intersection of these two planes marks the location of the side pocket.

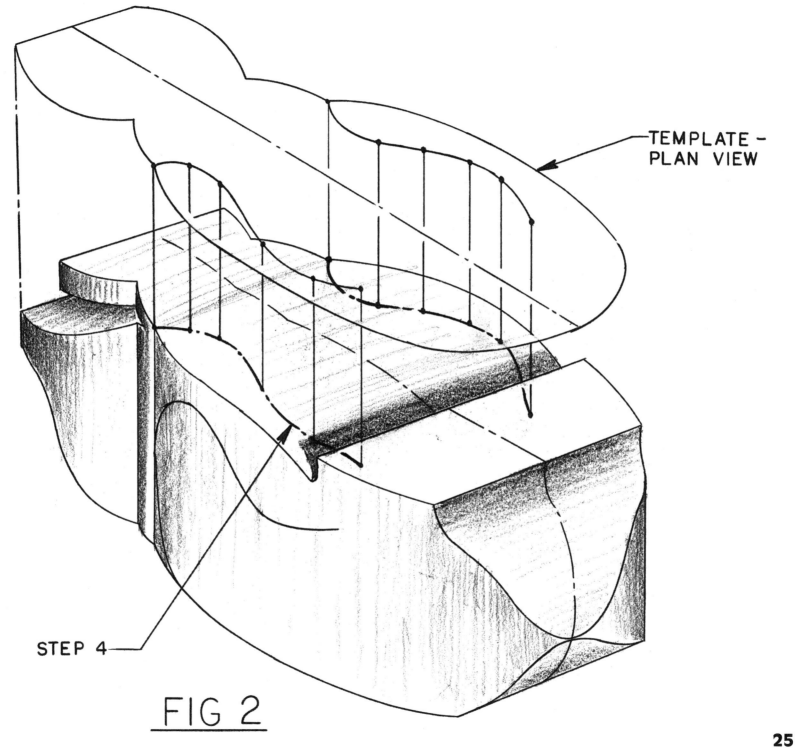

TEMPLATE - PLAN VIEW

STEP 4

FIG 2

25

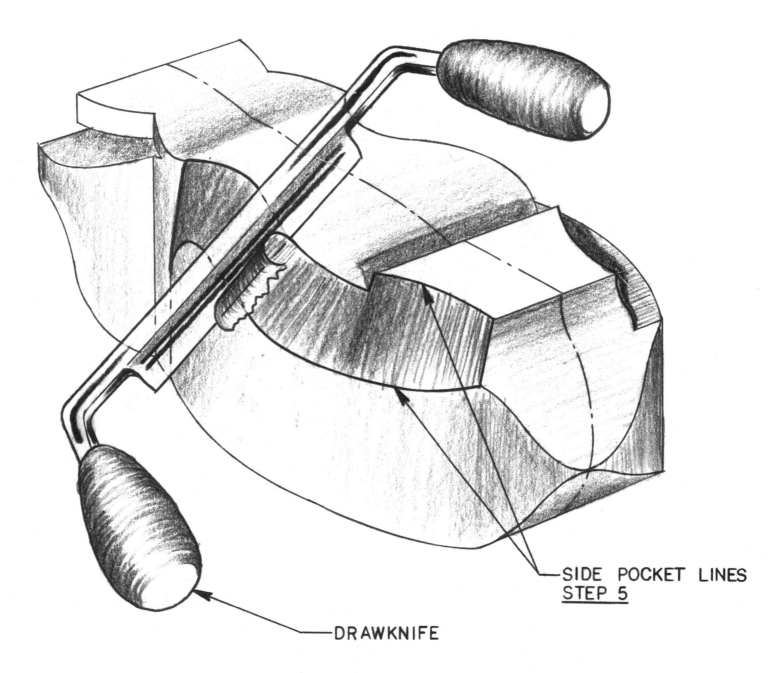

SIDE POCKET LINES
STEP 5

DRAWKNIFE

FIG 3

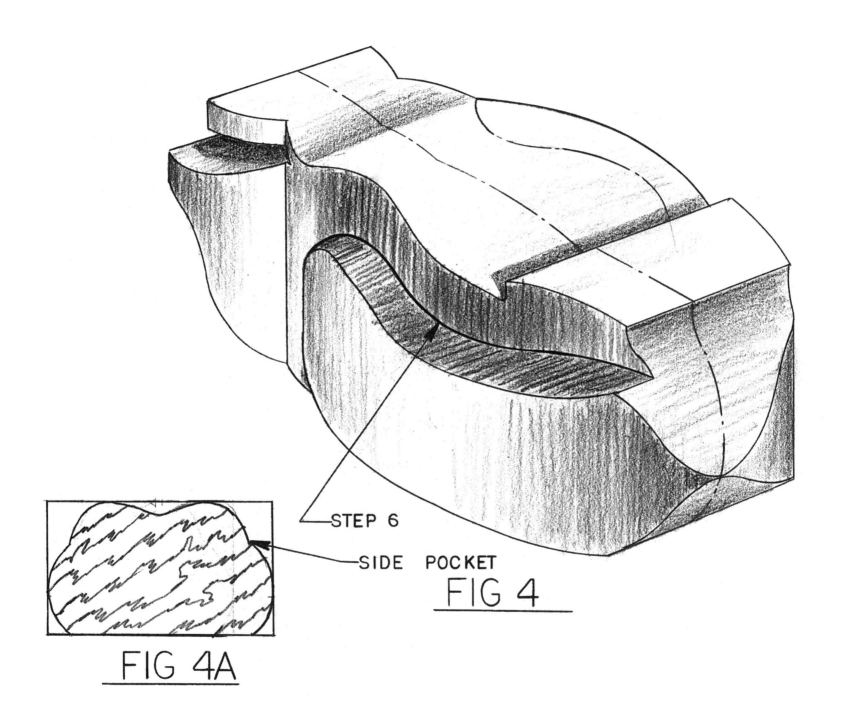

STEP 6

SIDE POCKET

FIG 4

FIG 4A

Step 7 Holding the blank upside down, draw an outline parallel to the outside of the blank. See Figure 5, page 29.

 Step 8 Starting at the bottom rear of the side pocket, create a step 5/16" deep at that point. Mark the point where Line A meets the side pocket line. See Point A, Figure 5, page 29. Continue carving the step along the side pocket line, gradually diminishing it to zero at Point A.

 Step 9 Hold the blank upside down. Start at the bottom of the 5/16" step created in Step 7, draw a line 9/16" long toward the center line. See Figure 5, page 29.

 Step 10 From the end of this 9/16" line draw a line toward the tail of the bird. This line should be parallel to the outside of the blank and curve toward the center line.

 Step 11 Draw another curved line forming an arc forward. This line starts at the end of the 9/16" line and blends in rapidly with the line created in Step 7.

 Step 11A Starting at Point B (Figure 5A, page 29) create a curved line forming an arc upward and outward to Point C on Line A.

 Step 12 Starting from the line created in Step 10, round off the flank outward and upward, creating in the rear view a curved crease denoting the rear and lower end of the side pocket. See Figure 5, page 29 and Figure 6, page 31.

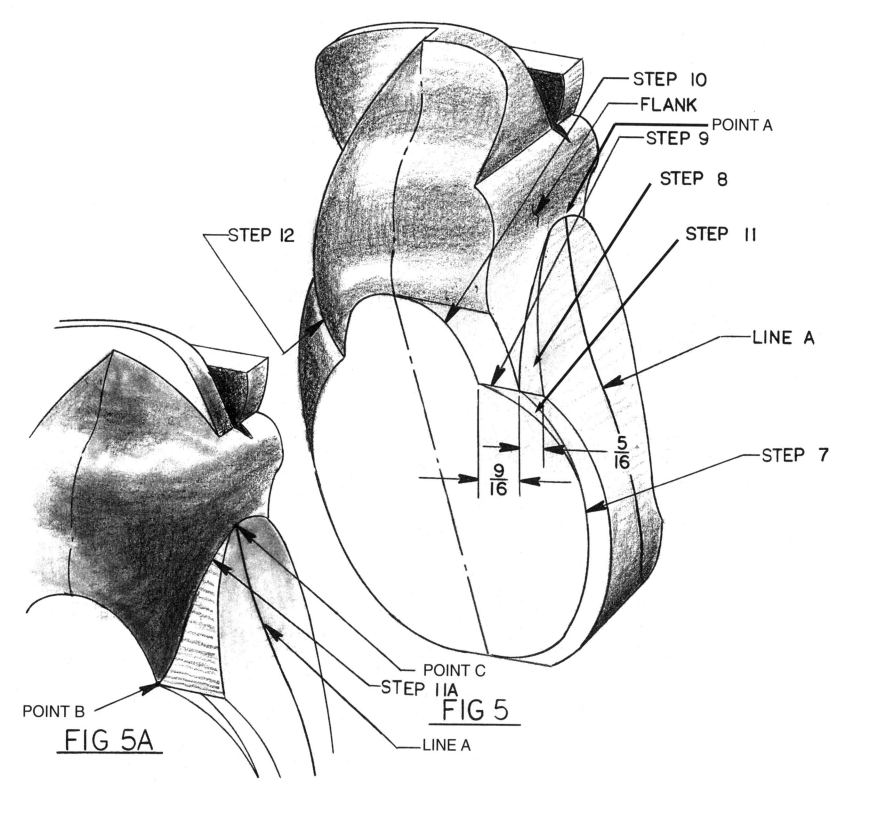

STEP 10

FLANK

POINT A

STEP 9

STEP 8

STEP 12

STEP 11

LINE A

STEP 7

$\frac{5}{16}$

$\frac{9}{16}$

POINT C

STEP 11A

FIG 5

LINE A

POINT B

FIG 5A

29

Step 13 Starting along the line at the base of the bird, round off toward the crease created in the previous step. Then round out the side pocket, outward and upward. See Figure 6, page 31. Also see Figure 4A, page 27, to determine the cross-sectional shape of the body.

Step 14 On the side of the blank, draw the line defining the outboard edge of the tail. See Figure 7, page 31.

Step 15 Using a small V-gouge, create the lower tail covert and define the tail plane. Keep a $1/8$" thickness for the tail. See Figure 6, page 31.

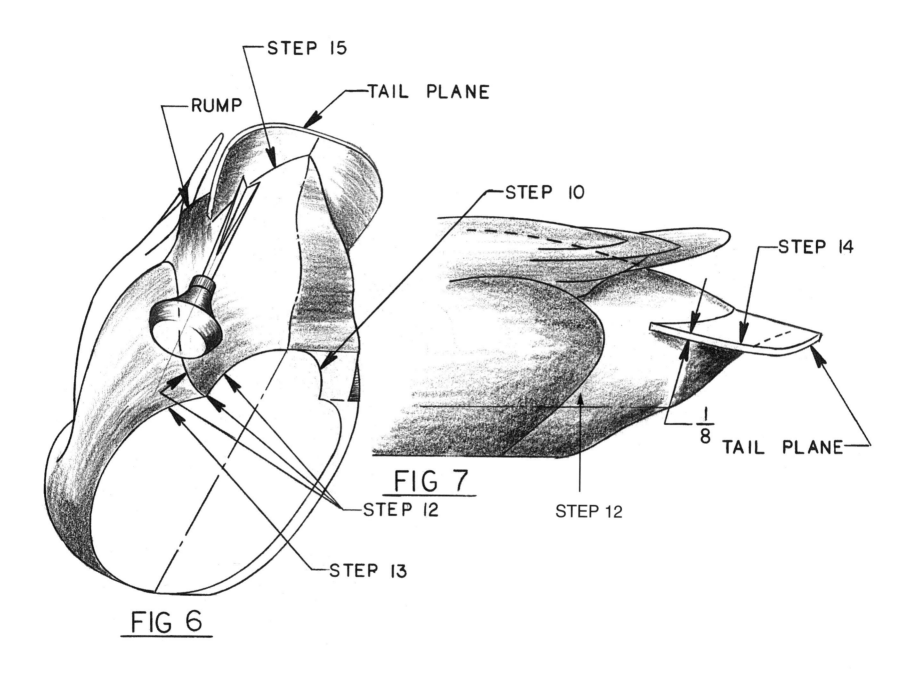

STEP 15

RUMP

TAIL PLANE

STEP 10

STEP 14

STEP 12

STEP 12

$\frac{1}{8}$ TAIL PLANE

FIG 7

STEP 13

FIG 6

Step 16   Round off the side pocket and back and shoulder areas to the side pocket line. See Figure 8, page 33.

Step 17   Using the drawing on page 7, draw the secondary feathers. From these lines rearward, round off the rump and upper plane of the tail section. Also create the upper tail coverts. See Figures 8 and 8A, page 33.

Step 18   Again, referring to the drawing on page 8, draw lines formed by the innermost edge of the tertials and primaries. Remove the wood from between these lines. Take care to maintain the proper rate of slope so this area blends in with the top of the rump. See Figures 8 and 8A, page 33.

Step 19   Using a small U-gouge, follow the center line from the point where the tertials meet at the rear of the body to the back of the neck. Make the groove $3/16"$ deep. Round off the edges of the groove. See Figures 8 and 8A, page 33.

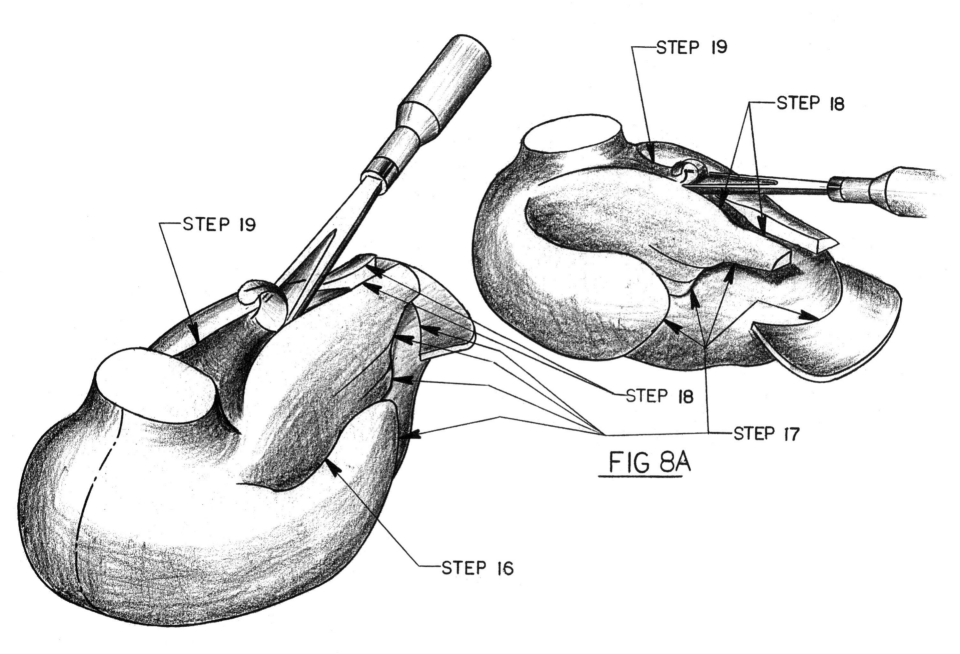

STEP 19

STEP 19

STEP 18

STEP 18

STEP 17

STEP 16

FIG 8A

FIG 8

33

Step 20   Temporarily attach the head to the body with a double-ended wood screw or a long wood screw. See Figure 9, page 35.

Step 21   Referring to Figure 10 from page 21 and Figure 9 from page 19, carve the neck area. Take care to achieve an "hour-glass" shape.

Step 22   Carve a groove with a U-gouge to separate the neck from the shoulder area. Blend in all areas on each side of that groove, taking care to define the neck and shoulder areas well. See Figure 9, page 35.

Step 23   Based on the feathering patterns shown on the drawings on page 8 and 9, lay out the feathers on the bird. Lay out the flow lines on the head and the breast. Maintaining a random pattern, establish the feather ends on the breast, rump, flank and undertail area, conforming to the flow lines. See Figure 9, page 35.

Step 24   Starting with the outboard tail feather, make a cut along the feather lines with an X-acto™ knife fitted with a #11 blade. Using a skew chisel, peel the wood next to the adjoining feather. See Figure 9, page 35, and also Figure 10 and Section A-A on page 37.

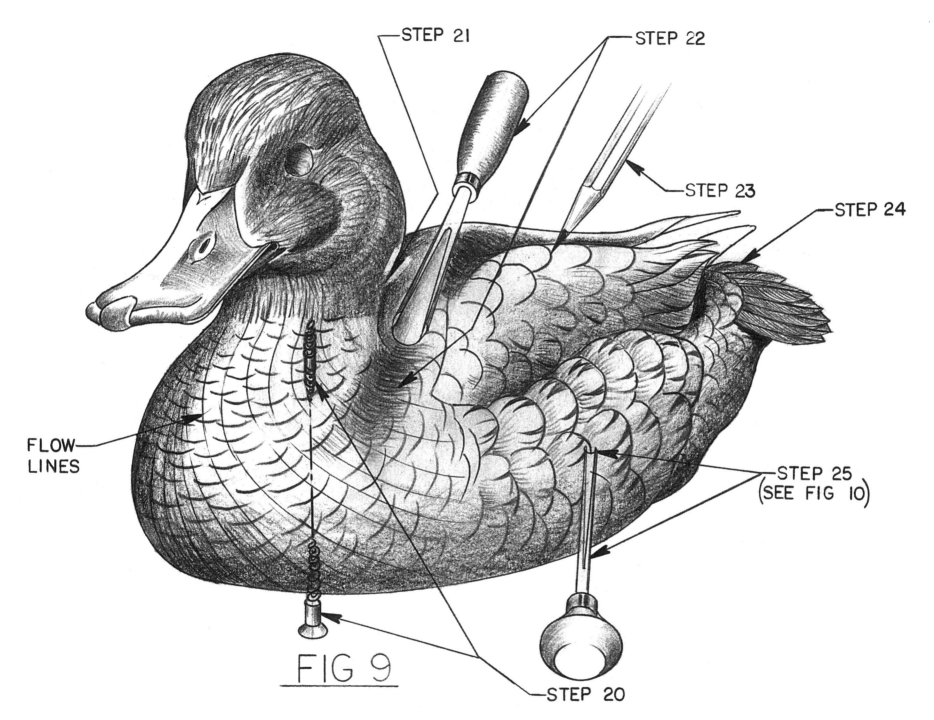

STEP 21

STEP 22

STEP 23

STEP 24

FLOW LINES

STEP 25
(SEE FIG 10)

FIG 9

STEP 20

35

Step 25   Using the same method used on the tail, proceed to carve all the feathers on the back and side of the bird, with the exception of the rump, flank, breast and undertail covert sections and the head.

 Note: Optional method to carve the side pocket feathers: Using a small U-gouge create a groove around each feather. Then go back and remove the sharp ridges left by the gouge by gently rolling the feather surface to the middle of the groove. See Figures 10A and 10B, page 37.

At this point, you can permanently fasten the head in place. Unscrew the head and apply a quick setting two-part epoxy to the joint surface. Screw the head on and tighten securely. Remove any excess glue that might ooze out.

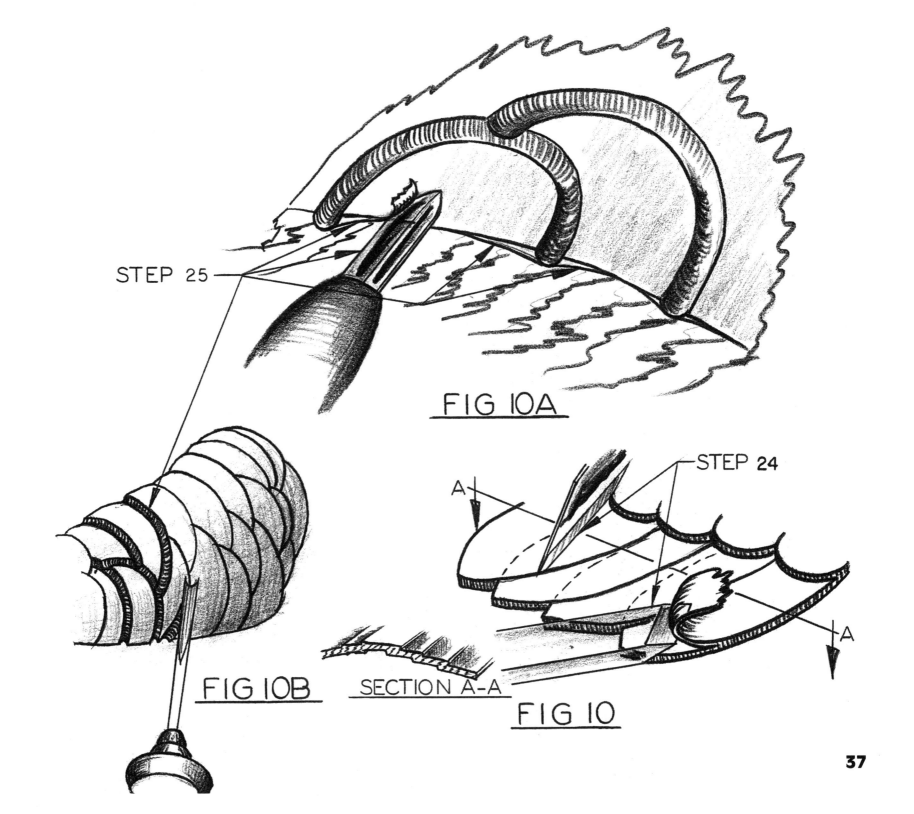

STEP 25

FIG 10A

STEP 24

FIG 10B

SECTION A-A

FIG 10

A

A

EYES

Use 8mm yellow glass eyes, available at a taxidermist supply.

Step 26   Drill a counter bore the diameter of the eye, deep enough so that one-third of the eye will protrude. Fill the cavity with wood filler and insert the eye. Cover all but the very center of the eye with this same material, making sure that you work it well into the wood. Allow it to dry thoroughly. See Figure 11, page 39.

Step 27   With an X-acto™ blade, cut the dried material over the eye to create an elliptical opening. Take care not to use too much pressure or you might score the eye. The material that remains will be used to form the eyelid. See Figure 11A, page 39.

Step 28   Using a very small U-gouge, form a groove on the eyelid material as shown in Figure 11B, page 39.

Now that the carving is completed, sand the whole bird with fine sandpaper.
Take care not to scratch the eyes.

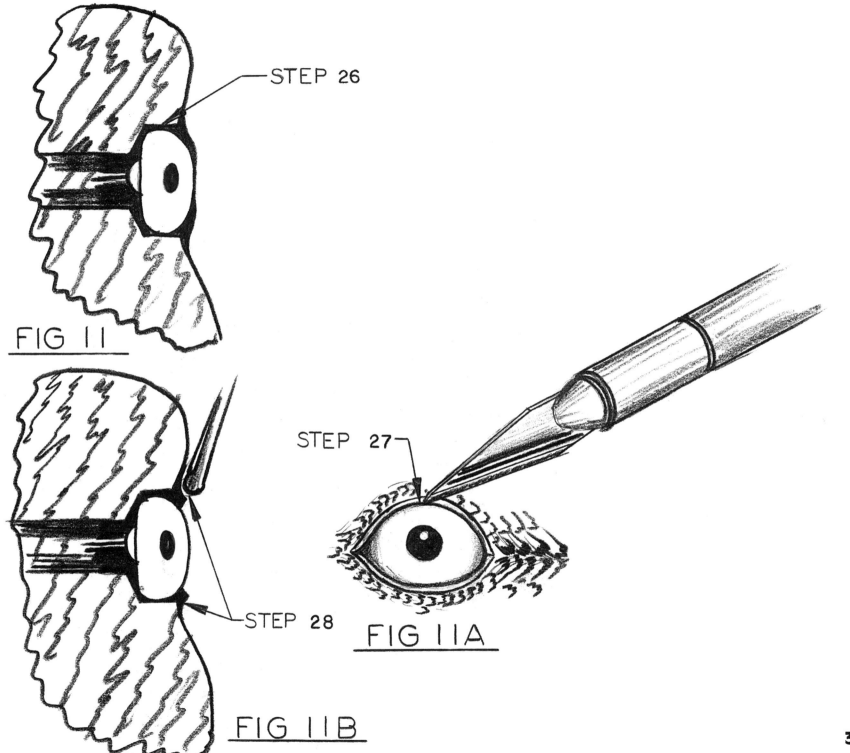

STEP 26

FIG 11

STEP 27

FIG 11A

STEP 28

FIG 11B

39

Figure 12 on page 41 shows the different types of textures required for a given group of feathers. Applying these different textures will allow you to achieve a more realistic-looking bird.

Step 29   In this operation, burn the shaft of the feather. This will be done to all the tail feathers, tertials and primaries. It is accomplished by carefully burning two lines close together that come to a point at the tip of the feather. A little practice here on a scrap piece of wood is helpful. See Figure 12A, page 41.

Step 30   Here again, practice is very beneficial. Once you feel confident with the burning tool, begin to texture the tail, starting with the outboard feather and working toward the center line. Make your texture as it appears in Figure 12B, page 41. Take care that each burned line is arced as shown, and not straight. Do not make the feather look like a Christmas tree.

Step 31   Proceed in this same manner to the tertials. See Figure 12C, page 41.

Step 32   The tail coverts, rump, flanks and breast feathers receive a different treatment. Once your feathers have been laid out as in Step 23, Figure 9, page 35, begin burning the most forward feather in that particular feather group, as shown in Figure 12D, page 41. To texture the feather covered by the one just completed, bring the tip of the burning tool to the end of the previous feather, and apply a tiny amount of pressure. Then continue your stroke, gradually decreasing pressure. The effect you will get is that the first feather will appear to be covering the second feather, even though no feather was carved.

Step 33   The head and neck are textured very much like the feathers in the step above. These feathers are much smaller, especially near the bill and gradually get larger toward the back of the head and neck area. Carefully study Figure 12 and 12E, page 41 to see the shape and pattern of these feathers. Care should be taken not to obtain a pattern, but rather a random effect. You do not want your feathers to appear as even rows, such as corn rows.

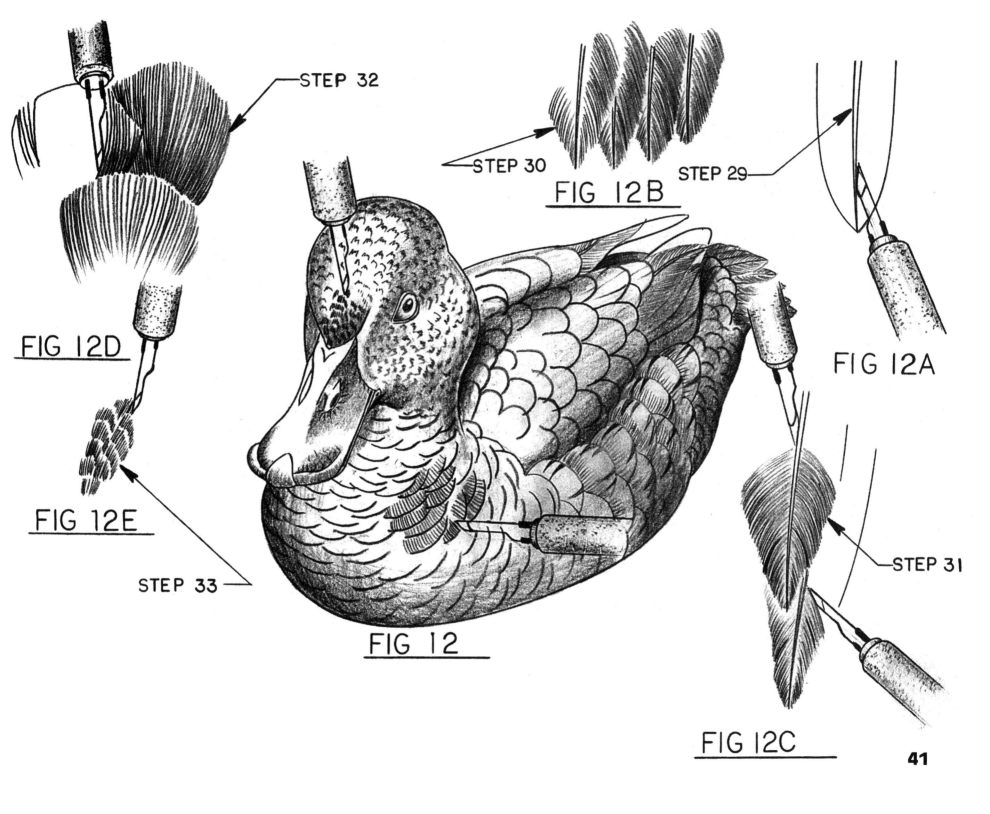

STEP 32

STEP 30

FIG 12B

STEP 29

FIG 12A

FIG 12D

FIG 12E

STEP 33

STEP 31

FIG 12

FIG 12C

PAINTING INSTRUCTIONS

A paint pattern and color guide are shown on the inside and back covers. Refer to them as you read this section on painting.

Sealing and Priming

Once you have finished texturing the bird, use a stiff tooth brush to vigorously brush the bird in the direction of the texture. Seal the carving with a lacquer-based sanding sealer thinned with 50 percent lacquer thinner. Apply 2 or 3 thin coats, brushing the bird between coats with the tooth brush.

With a stiff brush, apply gesso thinned with 50 percent water to the whole bird. Work in the direction of the texture and make sure that everything is covered. Apply two or three thin coats. This will provide you with a good surface on which to paint. Use a hair dryer to dry the gesso between coats.

Most or all of the painting will be done with paints diluted with water to a thin consistency. In almost every case you will also be using "washes." To obtain a wash consistency, add more water to the already thin mixture. Washes will be used to bring the different values of color together on each feather.

In each case, look at the paint pattern and chart on the inside and back covers to determine the colors and the feathers to be painted. I always start with the tail and work my way forward. First, I apply one or two thin coats of the primer color. In the case of the dark areas on this carving, Color A is the primer. Then I start rendering each feather individually with the color designated for that group.

Rendering Individual Feathers

To render individual feathers, I apply the color with a semi-dry, round brush, and I try to achieve a variegated appearance. I try to deposit more paint on the outer edges and tips of each feather, graduating to less paint on the interior of the feather. The whole idea is to attempt to create a graduated look which will tend to resemble the real feather. Every feather will then be made up of different values by virtue of the amount of layers of paint applied on the outside of the feather compared to fewer layers on the inside. Once the desired intensity of the color is achieved, apply a thin wash of the same color over the whole group to bring all of the values closer together.

When I paint feathers, I try to achieve, in order to mimic nature, several values of the same color on each feather. I start by painting the whole area with a layer of the color, having a consistency which will permit the paint to flow, but not cover in one coat. If the paint is too thick, it will not look right and will fill in the carved details. A more natural appearance is achieved by applying several thin layers, with a semi-dry brush. I concentrate the pigment near the edges and tip of a feather and gradually deposit less as I move to the interior of the feather. Once I am satisfied I have the right color and appearance, I apply one or more washes of the same color to that area to bring all of the values together, creating a pleasant-looking painting.

Tail

Apply one or two coats of Color A over the whole tail using a #4 or #5 round sable brush. Start applying Color B in several layers with a semi-dry brush. Concentrate on depositing the paint on the outside and tip of each feather, then taper to no paint being applied on the inside of the feather. Repeat the process with each feather until the desired color is achieved. Apply one or more washes of Color B until all of the values are brought closer together.

Primaries

Apply Color A to the complete primaries. Using Color B apply paint over the primaries and render as in the tail, above. Once the desired effect is achieved, add some white to the mixture and edge each primary.

Upper and Lower Tail Coverts and Rump

Apply Color A to the whole area. Apply Color C in the same manner as in the tail. Once all the feathers are rendered according to the illustration, wash over the whole area with the same color until the desired effect is achieved. Using a #2 pointed sable brush or equivalent, detail the edges of the coverts by individually extending barbs into the tail.

Tertials and Secondaries

Apply Color A to the whole area. Using Color D, paint tertials and secondaries in a similar manner. Once completed, show the vermiculation of the tertials with Color E.

Scapulars, Cape and Side Pockets

Apply Color E to the scapulars, cape and side pockets. Adding tiny amounts of nimbus grey and opal to Color E, shade the outer edges of all these feathers with this mixture. Vermiculate the side pockets with Color J. Vermiculate the cape and tertials with Color F.

Breast, Head and Neck

Apply Color A to the breast, head and neck. Detail individual feathers as before with Color F. Wash with the same color to bring values together. With a #2 pointed sable, draw individual barbs onto the side pockets and cape. Add some white to Color F and highlight head as shown with a dry brush. Make a wash of Color G and apply it to the head and neck.

Bill

Apply Color H to the bill until it is covered. Shade with Color I, very thin, with semi-dry brush. Use warm white, very thin , and a semi-dry brush to highlight. Repeat until the desired effect is achieved. Apply Color F to the nail.

EXPLANATION OF TERMS AND PAINTING TECHNIQUES

Wash: A very thin and transparent application of paint, usually the same color as that being washed over.

Rendering: The act of detailing and sharpening details on the painting.

Dry Brush: Using a very thin portion of paint, the brush is wiped dry or until the paint skips on a piece of paper. There is enough paint left in the brush to do some fine detailing such as highlighting and shading.

Value: The variation of intensity in a color. Using the very same color, applied in very thin layers, graduating from several layers near the edge and top to a few layers at the center of the feather.

Highlighting: Usually adding white to a color and applying it so as to "bring out" certain portions of painting, usually parts of the anatomy where light would hit first.

Shading: Adding darker values of a color to an area which is not directly in the path of light, such as areas in shadows.

Vermiculation: Using the colors recommended for each area, and using a #2 pointed sable brush, apply series of dashes, as in painting, in a zig-zag pattern. Each succeeding row runs somewhat parallel to the preceding one.

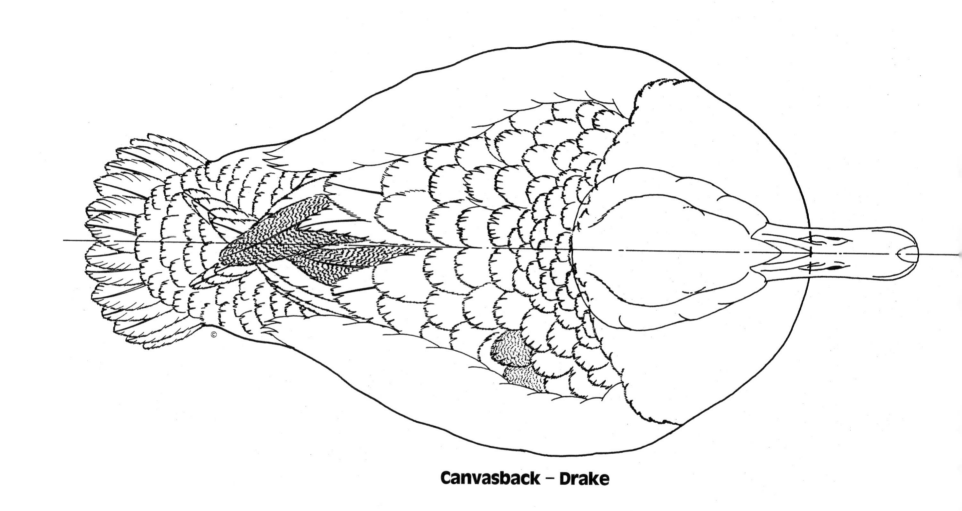

Canvasback – Drake

Enlarge 150%

46

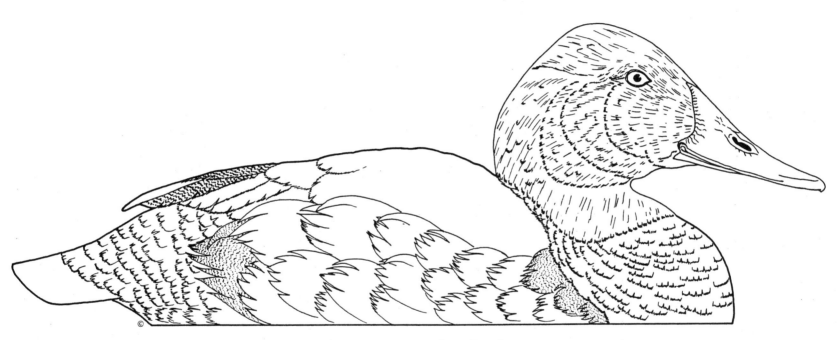

Canvasback – Drake

Enlarge 150%

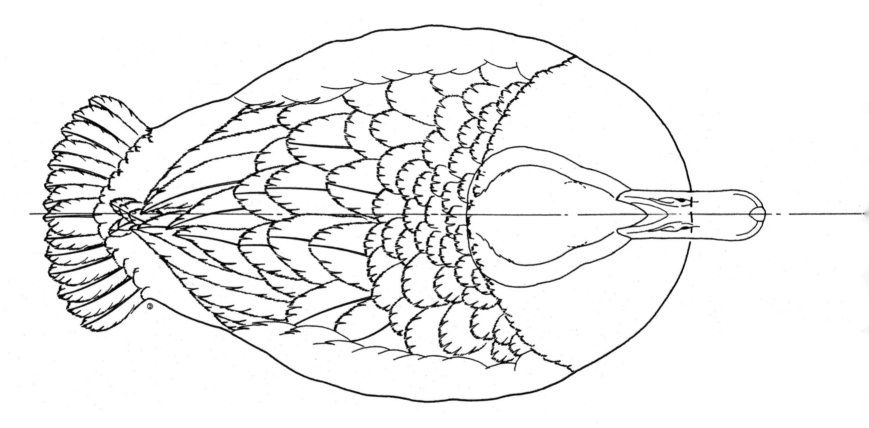

Canvasback – Hen

Enlarge 150%

48

Canvasback – Hen

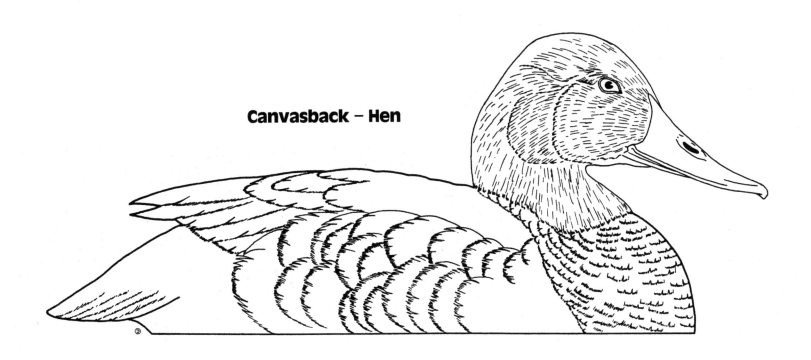

Enlarge 150%

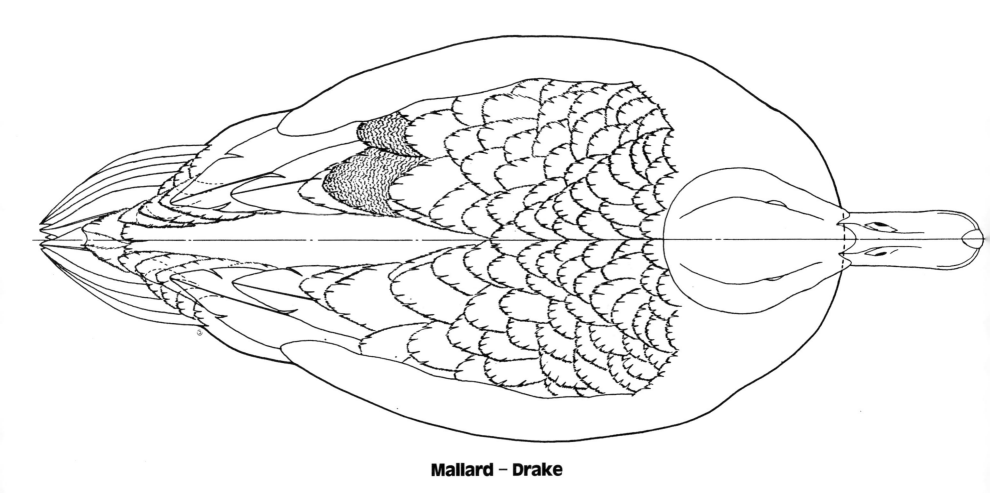

Mallard – Drake

Enlarge 158%

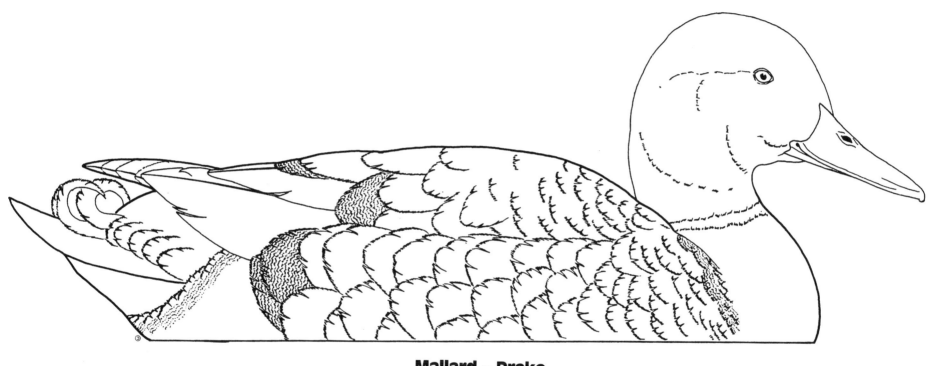

Mallard – Drake

Enlarge 158%

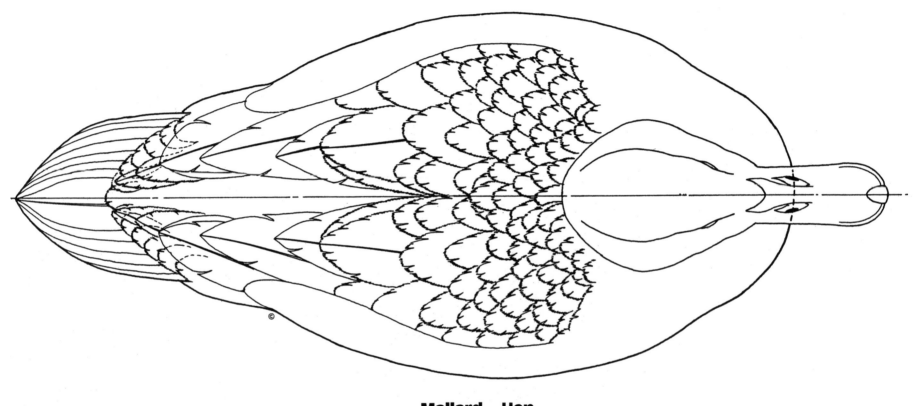

Mallard – Hen

Enlarge 150%

Mallard – Hen

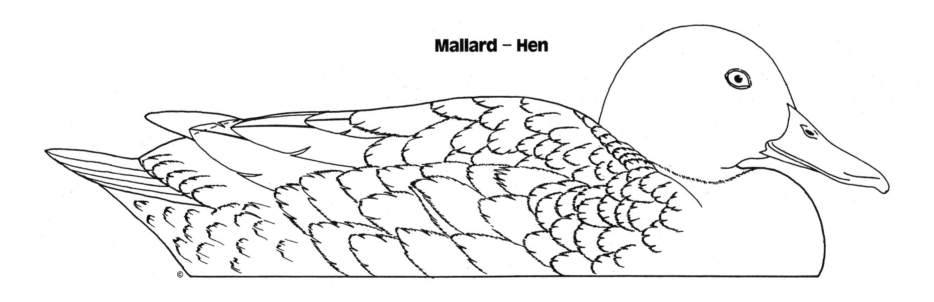

Enlarge 150%

Afterword

What I hoped to accomplish with this book was to give everyone with a desire to carve a realistic duck as comprehensive a set of instructions as needed to make it almost impossible to fail. I sincerely hope I have succeeded. If this book provides you with half the enjoyment that bird carving has provided for me, than I am satisfied that I have reached my goal. If you have never carved a duck before, you will be richly rewarded by your experience.

Since the original printing of *Realistic Duck Carving,* I have written two other books: *26 Realistic Duck Patterns,* which contains full-size patterns with feather details of males and females for $23.50 including shipping and handling; and *Favorite Bird Patterns,* which deals with many different birds and is $20 including shipping and handling. Both the books are available from Bird Sculptures in Wood, 3825 Dearborn Ave., Rochester Hills, MI 48309.

God bless you in your endeavors.

Al

P.S. I can't over-emphasize the need to practice extreme caution in performing a lot of the steps in this book using very sharp tools. Safety should always be foremost in mind when a tool is in your hand.

You are invited to Join the

National Wood Carvers Association
"Some carve their careers: others just chisel"
since 1953

If you have any interest in woodcarving: if you carve wood, create wood sculpture or even just whittle in your spare time, you will enjoy your membership in the National Wood Carvers Association. The non-profit NWCA is the world's largest carving club with over 33,000 members. There are NWCA members in more than 56 countries around the globe.

The Association's goals are to:
- promote wood carving
- foster fellowship among member enthusiasts
- encourage exhibitions and area get togethers
- list sources of equipment and information for the wood carving artist
- provide a forum for carving artists

The NWCA serves as a valuable network of tips, hints and helpful information for the wood carver. Membership is only $11.00 per year.

Members receive the magazine "Chip Chats" six times a year, free with their membership. "Chip Chats" contains articles, news events, demonstrations of technique, patterns and a full color section showcasing examples of fine craftsmanship. Through this magazine you will be kept up to date on shows and workshops to attend, new products, special offers to NWCA members and other members' activities in your area and around the world.

National Wood Carvers Association
7424 Miami Ave.
Cincinnati, OH 45243

Name: _____

Address: _____

_____

Dues $11.00 per year in USA, $14.00 per year foreign (payable in US Funds)

 FOX BOOKS

Titles From Fox Chapel Publishing

DESIREE HAJNY TITLES

Big Cats by Desiree Hajny
Carving Lions, Tigers and Jaguars. Desi's new full color guide to carving these majestic predators. 100's of color photos and anatomy charts guide you through creating your own masterpiece. Also features painting instructions and reference photos of live animals.
$14.95

Mammals: An Artistic Approach by Desiree Hajny (second printing)
Carvers will learn to carve realistic North American mammals - deer, bear and otter in this informative 150 page book. Carving techniques for both hand tool and powercarvers are covered plus much needed info on texturing, woodburning and painting.
$19.95

Carving Caricature Animals by Desiree Hajny
Learn how to make caricature carvings based on real animals. Desi shows you how to use cartooning techniques to emphasize an animal's most recognizable characteristics – and then turn those ideas into a caricature carving. Includes over 100 color photos, step-by-step carving and painting techniques, and patterns.
$14.95

Carving Small Animals
In this comprehensive book, Desi includes everything you'll need to carve rabbits, racoons and squirrels. Anatomy sketches, descriptions of the animals, and reference photos give you a detailed look at your subject. Charts and photos outline techinques for carving and painting in a step-by-step fashion. Includes patterns, too!
$14.95

MARY DUKE GULDAN TITLES

Mary Duke Guldan has been writing and illustrating the ¡Lets Carve¡ column here in Chip Chats for over a decade. The books below offer expanded and revised material.

Woodcarver's Workbook Carving Animals with Mary Duke Guldan
Called the "best woodcarving pattern book in 40 years" by NWCA president Ed Gallenstein. Carving instructions and detailed information on 9 realistic projects including dogs, moose, wolves, whitetail deer, wild horses & more.
$14.95

Woodcarver's Workbook #2
All new projects (no repeats from book #1 above). Projects inside: Native Indian Chief, buffalo, elk, horses, mules, cattle and oxen, plus a country farmer pattern.
$14.95

CARICATURE CARVERS OF AMERICA (CCA)

Carving The Full Moon Saloon
Caricature carvers will delight in the work of this group of great carvers. 21 members including well known teachers like Harold Enlow, Claude Bolton, Steve Prescott, Desiree Hajny, Tom Wolfe and Jack Price. Together, these members created "The Full Moon Saloon" a scale model measuring 4 feet long and containing over 40 carvings. Carving the Full Moon Saloon is a 120 page color guide to the creative work involved in these characters. Close up photos show incredible details. Includes patterns and painting technique section.

THE book for Caricature Carvers	$19.95
Hardcover edition (quantities limited)	$29.95

STEVE PRESCOTT TITLES

Carving Blockheads by Steve Prescott
What is a Blockhead? A Blockhead is a basic shape roughout that can be carved into infinite character-filled personalities. Join Steve as he carves a basic blockhead and then features patterns and color photos of 50 more Blockheads - doctors, nurses, policeman, gnomes...and many more. An exciting new look at carving!
$12.95

Cowtown Carving Carving Characters with Texas Whittling Champion Steve Prescott.
15 projects including Cowtown Santa, Rodeo Clown and lots of cowboys! Steve includes both a full size bandsaw roughout pattern and a detail pattern for each project. Good pattern book for the intermediate + carver.
$14.95

Whittling Old Sea Captain and Crew by Mike Shipley
An exciting book on caricature style from this Ozarks Mountain carver. Over 100 photos and color painting guide plus patterns.
$12.95

JIM MAXWELL TITLES

Ozarks carver Jim Maxwell has been teaching and carving around Branson, MO for over 25 years. Jim's work shows clean lines, smooth finish and original patterns. Recently, we've started producing roughouts (see below) of his most popular projects.

Carving Clowns with Jim Maxwell
Over 200 b/w and color photos introduce you to the humorous world of clowns. Complete how to information for carving and painting. Patterns for 12 different clowns included inside. Highly Recommended!
$14.95

Woodcarving Adventure Movie Characters
An excellent how to carve book using characters from Jim's favorite silver screen heroes as inspiration. Carve a sailor, cowboy or 21 other exciting characters. All patterns included inside. Over 150 step-by-step photos.
$12.95

Carving Characters
12 favorite projects including Jim's famous Turkey Buzzard.
$6.95

Making Collectible Santas and Christmas Ornaments
8 creative Santas and 34 ornament patterns.
$6.95

Maxwell Roughouts

(#RO1)	Roly Poly Santa (5") tall,	$6.00
(#RO2)	Snowman (4") tall,	$6.00
(#RO3)	Butterfly Catcher (Emmett Kelley-type) 10" tall,	$15.00
(#RO4)	Auguste - style - classic clown style 8" tall,	$15.00

BIRD CARVING TITLES

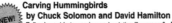

Carving Hummingbirds by Chuck Solomon and David Hamilton
Full color guide to carving and painting "hummers". Patterns for broadtail and ruby throat included. 100's of photos in full color. Reference material on anatomy, wings and habitat. Highly Recommended!
$19.95

GEORGE LEHMAN CARVING PATTERN BOOKS

Minnesota carver George Lehman's pattern books are a very useful source for beginning and intermediate carvers. Tips, sketches and techniques are sprinkled throughout each book. Four volumes available:

Book One: Carving 20 Realistic Game and Songbirds
Partial list: common loon, chickadee, owl, mallard, grouse, robin, pintails.
$19.95

Book Two: Realism in Wood
Partial list: bald eagle, kingfisher, pheasants, bobwhite, great horned owl, pileated woodpecker, red-tailed hawk, mockingbird.
$19.95

Book Three: Nature in Wood
Partial list: barnswallow, cardinal, warblers (3), wrens, goldfinch + 10 animal patterns.
$16.95

Book Four: Carving Wildlife in Wood
Partial list: Canada goose, wild turkey, osprey, Baltimore oriole, great blue heron.
$19.95

Encyclopedia of Bird Reference Drawings by David Mohardt
Detailed sketches, wing studies and reference info for carvers. 215 different varieties of birds covered. Recommended by Larry Barth, Bob Guge.
$14.95

Carving Fish - Miniature Salt water and Freshwater by Jim Jensen
These detailed patterns, woodburning tips, color painting sections and step-by-step photos show you how to carve 26 different miniature fish for sale or display.
$14.95

Carousel Horse Carving
An instruction workbook by Ken Hughes. Recommended as a classic how-to on carving carousel horses. Ken shows you everything step-by-step in making a denzel style carving in 1/3 standard size. Over 150 photos. New edition includes full size fold out pattern.
$24.95

Carving Vermont Folk Figures with Power
by Frank Russell, the Author of "Carving Realistic Animals with Power" offers an exciting collection of characters from The Bachelor to The Logger ready to use patterns included.
$9.95

Fantastic Book of Canes, Pipes and Walking Sticks by Harry Ameredes
This WV Artist and carver has made canes simple and decorative for over 30 years. In these hundred of detailed drawings you'll find lots of ideas for canes, weathered wood and pipes. Plus info on collecting tree roots.
$12.95

Bark Carving by Joyce Buchanan
Learn to harvest and carve faces - mystical woodspirits and other expressions in bark colorful guide with pattern and lots of helpful info.
$12.95

Sculpturing Totem Poles by Walt Way
Easy to follow pattern and instruction manual. Lots of clear drawings plus three patterns inside.
$6.95

Carving Wooden Critters
Diane Ernst carves appealing animals that are best described as realistic caricatures. 16 high quality patterns for rabbits, puppies, otters and more.
$6.95

JUDY GALE ROBERTS INTARSIA BOOKS

Intarsia is a way of making picture mosaics in wood using 3/4 lumber. Carvers can further enhance their intarsia pieces by selective detailing.

Easy to Make Inlay Wood Projects
The best introduction to intarsia. Over 100 photos show you how it is done. Also includes 12 free patterns and 30 color photos.
$19.95

Small Intarsia Projects
Full color guide with 12 patterns for a wide variety of pieces.
$14.95

300 Christian and Inspirational Designs
Although written for scroll saw users, this book will be most helpful for carvers looking for designs to carve both in relief and in the round. $14.95

Mott Miniature Furniture Workshop Manual
Ready to use pattern for 144 scale model furniture projects. Best book on the subject.
$19.95

TOLL FREE 1-800-457-9112

HOW TO ORDER:
CREDIT CARD ORDERS MAY CALL **1-800-457-9112**
MAIL ORDERS PLEASE SEND BOOK PRICE PLUS $2.50 PER BOOK
(MAXIMUM $5 SHIPPING CHARGE) TO:

Fox Chapel Publishing • 1970 Broad Street • East Petersburg, PA 17520 • FAX (717) 560-4702

Dealers write or call for wholesale listing of over 800 titles on woodworking and carving